YOGITRIATHLETE
COOKBOOK

High Vibe Recipes for the Athlete Appetite

JESS GUMKOWSKI

DESIGN & PHOTOGRAPHY BY: BJ GUMKOWSKI

2017

YogiTriathlete

Carlsbad, California 92008

YogiTriathlete.com

INGREDIENTS

Disclaimer: Recipes, wellness tips and nutrition advice is not meant to treat or cure any medical condition or disease. Always consult with your doctor about your personal health and wellness. We are not Registered Dietitians. Jess is a Vegan Lifestyle Coach and Educator and BJ is certified in Plant-Based Nutrition from the T. Colin Campbell Center of Nutrition Studies. All reviews are strictly personal opinion. Always do your own research on products and companies before using a product on the internet. YogiTriathlete does not claim responsibility for any of the products, books, or companies discussed in this book. All content is meant to inspire others towards a more balanced, healthy and happy life.

This book is dedicated to our moms,
Joan and Teri.

For the thousands of homemade, whole-food meals that you
prepared with love and served with kindness despite
our behavior and awkward stages of growth.

Thank you moms, we love you!

Acknowledgements

To my soul sisters Lynda and Tara, thank you for sharing your gifts
and for your loving generosity to be in service of this project.
And to my husband, soulmate and warrior partner, for your willingness to
taste test every recipe a million times, design the book and capture the
goregous essence of these dishes,
I thank you.

MEET THE HIGH VIBERS

JESS GUMKOWSKI

Head Yogi
Recipe Creator and Author

Jess became a triathlete in September 2005, a year after saying that she would "never, ever do a triathlon... ever". Since finishing her first sprint tri in Fort Collins, CO she has gone on to complete countless (as in too many to count) races including multiple Ironmans, half Ironmans, Olympics, Sprints, Marathons, Half Marathons, 10ks and 5ks.

Most recently she moved into the Ultra Marathon distance and it was love at first finish line. She's been training and racing for over a decade and before that, she began her relationship with yoga. A courtship with the ancient science of the mind that dates back to spring break 1993 when Jess rolled out her mat for the very first time in Kingston, Jamaica. Unbeknownst to her that day, YogiTriathlete was officially in the making.

A lifelong high vibe connoisseur, Jess has always trusted her intuitive voice and been in touch with the signs from the universe. She grew up in a household with a mom, Joan, who rarely used recipes. Joan worked full-time yet always seemed to be able to get dinner on the table at the same time every night. She would gaze into the refrigerator as if to have a silent conversation with its contents and then just like that, she would pull out item after item that somehow became that evening's dinner.

Not long into her independent years, Jess found herself with those same libertarian ways when it came to cooking and has always been able to produce a well-balanced meal without stress. As a seasoned endurance athlete she knows how important fueling the body is to successfully completing her training, getting to the starting line healthy and powering her recovery.

She is the designated preparer of food in her household and despite carrying a hefty training and work schedule (entrepreneurs are never off the clock), she has figured out a way to put a nutritious plant-based meal on the table every night except on the rare occasion when Jess and BJ eat out. She is committed to bringing her spiritual practice into the kitchen and infusing every dish with love. She believes that the energy of the preparer has everything to do with the nutrition of the food served and so for Jess, it's high vibe all the way.

Jess is a Vegan Lifestyle Coach and Educator and she believes that performance starts with simple, whole-food combinations that are for the good of all: the planet, the animals and the athletes.

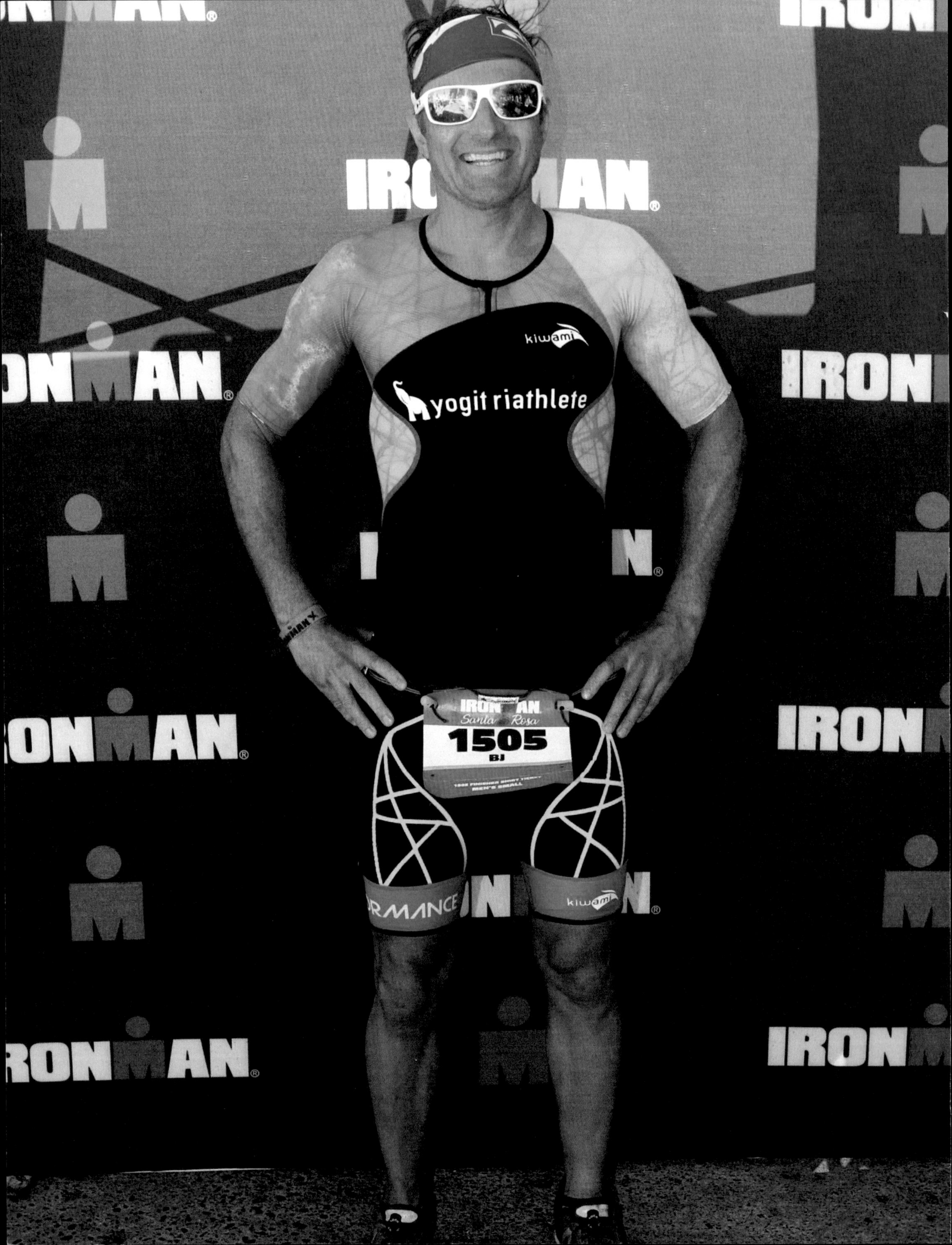
IRONMAN
kiwami
yogitriathlete
IRONMAN Santa Rosa
1505
BJ

BJ GUMKOWSKI

Head Triathlete
Book Photographer and Designer

While the other kids were out playing, BJ recalls patiently grinding away tomatoes from the backyard garden in preparation for his mother's homemade pasta sauce. After stocking the "hundreds" (maybe an exaggeration) of glass jars on the basement shelves, he was released to play to his heart's content. That was, of course, until he was called back to the garden to weed and sort rocks.

There's no wonder that BJ can sit on the bike trainer for 100 miles at a time, run a one-mile loop for hours in training and swim 10K by himself on his birthday every year with enthusiasm. This guy was meant for endurance sports and embracing discomfort. With the introduction of yoga and meditation into his training, his mental strength far surpasses that of his competitors. A multi-time Ironman with Kona qualification set deep within his heart, BJ holds a true love for the sport of triathlon.

His first triathlon in 2004 was complete with sub-55 degree water temps and a full-blown panic attack on the swim but that didn't stop BJ from firing his body across the finish line and into what has become a radiant element in his life's purpose. As a triathlon and running coach, BJ's passion for sport and the success of all those around him authentically comes across when working with his athletes. He lights up when serving others, assisting them to break through their limits, replace old belief systems with powerful commitments to move forward, and empower them to take a warrior stance in the face of all life's challenges.

Now certified in Plant-Based Nutrition from the T. Colin Campbell Center for Nutrition Studies, BJ not only thrives on a full spectrum plant-based diet, he works with athletes and non-athletes alike to incorporate more plants and mindfulness into their lives. He sees food as fuel. It's an everyday stepping stone to propel him closer to reaching his dreams and a choice that is good for our planet. On the cusp of "middle age", BJ continues to get faster and stronger every year practicing his recipe for success; mind, body and spirit.

ABOUT THE RECIPES

Eating a high vibrational diet is not something that I am willing to give up so I need to be smart with the time I have to spend on preparation and clean up. The majority of these recipes were born from that mindset. There are a few that take more time than others but I promise you I wouldn't have included them if they weren't completely worth it (i.e Coconut Banana Bread with Cacao Hazelnut Spread - wha???).

YogiTriathlete recipes don't break the bank or have hard-to-find ingredients and I assure you each creation is infused with love. This book was an absolute joy to compile. As you enjoy the meals, be inventive, make them your own, chew each bite and share with someone you love.

Progress Not Perfection

I don't pretend to be a gourmet chef. What I am is a triathlete, ultra-runner, yogi, podcaster, teacher, author (as soon as this book is published), wife, daughter, sister, friend and natural born seeker looking, finding and living my purpose. What I believe in when it comes to nutrition is easy to prepare, high vibrational, non-violent, plant-based meals that nourish mind, body and spirit in the midst of an adventurous life.

Sometimes that means using pre-made items like pizza crust, sauces etc. and that's ok, because it's about progress not perfection. It's about having vegan cheeseburger and fry night but then following up, or even better, preceeding that meal with a big ol' bowl of veggies. You'll notice that some of my recipes call for agave. I struggle with using agave because it's been shown to cause blood sugar levels to spike so I use it sparingly. If you are "beegan" than please replace all agave references with honey. There is balance to be had and consistent forward motion is what will allow that to unfold in your life so don't get stalled on every single detail. Do what feels right in your heart and remember progress, not perfection.

Mindful Eating

Most of these recipes are gluten-free or can be made gluten-free. BJ and I have not noticed sensitivities to eating gluten but we do tend to limit it in our daily diet. Also we don't have any food allergies so if you are sensitive to nuts or soy, these recipes are readily available for substitutes (rice milk for almond milk, sunflower seeds for walnuts).

Anaphylactic shock isn't the only result of food not agreeing with our bodies. Bloating, fatigue and skin irritation can all be signs that what we are putting in our bodies may not be in our highest good. Bringing awareness to our food choices is such a powerful exercise. It allows us to see what works and what doesn't work. We are all unique and with that, we are always changing.

Right now, as I write this and as you are reading this, there are cells birthing and dying in our bodies. We are never the same, our physiology is always changing. There are certain nutrients that our bodies require for optimal function but like perspective, it is particularly remarkable just how individual we are in our nutritional needs. In other words, pay attention on purpose, chew your food and listen to what your body is telling you. I've included a mindful eating section in this book to help you on your way to being awake and ready when you arrive to the plate. Move over zombies, there's a new sheriff in town and it's called mindfulness!

Portion Sizes

As an athlete, I tend to have an athlete appetite and as I prepare food for another athlete, our quantity needs are more than someone who is not on a training regime. As we move through our annual training programs, there are times where volume is high and volume is low, therefore our appetites adjust accordingly as our metabolisms react to our activity levels. Although this book is aimed at the athlete appetite, it is for everyone. It became obvious to me as I was having friends test these meals that BJ and I have large athlete appetites but one of the greatest things about eating plant-based is that the food keeps very well so there will be times when you will be getting two-for-ones (time saver bonus).

Restaurant Grade Kitchen Not Necessary

In June 2016, BJ and I (and Clark, our golden retriever) pulled out of the driveway of our dream home with everything we owned packed into our Honda Fit. After months of getting rid of almost everything, we were officially homeless. We hit the road that day with very little planned other than to raise awareness that living a more vibrant life is within reach for all and to never accumulate more than we need ever again.

When we landed in our now home of Carlsbad, California six months later, I upped our kitchen inventory with a few necessities like two bowls, two plates, two glasses, one mixing bowl, one loaf pan, one baking sheet and one baking dish. This collection of recipes were all created in a kitchen with one sautee pan, one medium sized pot, one cutting board, one knife and a reconditioned Vitamix* all of which made the initial cross-country trek. There is nothing special that you need for these recipes, just a willingness to infuse love into your meals and faith that there is time everyday to eat healthy.

*Vitamix sells certified reconditioned blenders for a fraction of the cost. Also a search using the phrase "affordable high powered blenders" on that super cool tool called Google may just surprise you.

HOW TO THRIVE

I love the movie, *The Kids Are All Right*. In it, Mark Ruffalo plays the gentle, unknowingly funny and noncommittal Paul, owner of an organic foods restaurant and anonymous sperm donor for two children. The premise of the movie is that Paul is found by said children and this is followed by several awkward attempts to get to know the children. Meanwhile a tense love triangle builds between Paul and the kids parents, lesbian couple Nic and Jules, played by Julieanne Moore and Annette Benning. It's a great movie, funny, touching, aggravating and sweet. If you haven't seen it, you should.

And this has what to do with thriving on a plant-based diet?

Well let me tell you, there is a scene where Paul and Joni, his sperm daughter, are in his organic garden and Paul picks a pepper from its source, tears it in half and offers it to Joni as they connect over a conversation about Nic. From the moment the pepper is torn open, I felt and heard its crispness, I sensed its essence of high vibe nutrition and I imagined sprays of water released from its insides with every bite. For me, it was an enviable moment where I just wanted to live the rest of my days in a garden under a pepper plant but the takeaway was the reminder that good nutrition is not complicated.

The fact is: eating healthy is simple, especially when it comes to plant foods. Mother nature created sustenance for the animals (yes, we are animals) that walk her earth in a way that is perfectly packaged in form and nutrient load. We have a tendency in our world to doubt this and to overanalyze the divine intelligence of mother nature's abundance. We question its validity and we scrutinize its supremacy to a point where we reduce down nutrition from a symphony to individual instruments. This is a carb. This is a protein. This is a fat. In essence, by dissecting, we dumb down the innate science of nutrition that is naturally provided by the earth.

In his book, *Approaching the Natural*, Sid Garza-Hillman notes that there are no nutrients that were created in isolation nor meant to be consumed in isolation. Plant foods truly are a symphony of nutrients meant to work in harmony with one another. So when you find yourself overthinking, revisit this section of the book and heed to the guidance of the following pillars to nutritional prosperity. This is how you will thrive.

Embrace What is True

The truth is, food is for fuel, nothing more. It can be medicine or poison, the choice is ours. Ask yourself this everyday and anytime you feel burdened in the kitchen: "What is more important than the food I put into my body?" Now follow up that question with this affirmation: "This is the foundational gasoline that fuels my body, my brain, my energy level, my athletic pursuits, my mood, my relationships, my sleep, my future, my life."

Take the emotion out of it and make choices based on truth and that are in alignment with your goals. If you must, write down your goals and post them on the fridge to serve as a reminder of your true desires. This will hold you accountable to making choices that are in alignment with your pursuits, athletic or otherwise. Food is for fuel, nothing more and that's the truth.

Eat the Spectrum

Years ago a friend of mine was talking about a children's nutrition book that she was writing and she said that the way she gets kids to understand healthy nutrition is through color. If the colors on your plate are beige or brown, start again. If your plate is colorful, go from there. Her message to the parents who were active in assisting their children to learn their way around the kitchen was simply to "cook with color".

When we cook with color, the nutritional levels of our meals are guaranteed to be high. A plant-based whole foods diet that spans the spectrum of options and color will give us the greatest shot at living in a healthy body. Stop passing by those odd options in the produce department as they are not odd to everyone and may only be odd to you. Regardless, Mother Nature didn't create them so they could go uneaten.

Instead of being afraid, get to know them, it will only take a few seconds. If you haven't heard, there's this uber informational tool called Google. Pull it up, punch in the name of this odd plant food and see the thousands of results on how to eat, prepare and cook said oddity. The great thing about Google is that it won't judge you and no one has to know you are learning something new. I get it, some people don't know how to serve zucchini, not to mention crazy stuff like jackfruit or plantains but remember, food is fuel and this odd-looking foe could just be the friend your body needs.

Shortcuts Are Worth It

I am a firm believer in convenience and I will pay for it. I am nothing without my health and as the primary preparer of food in my household, it is my job to uphold nutritional levels that are aligned with our highest good. It just so happens that our highest good is also aligned with the highest good of the earth and the other animals that live on it since we've decided not to eat them anymore.

Convenience costs and that's the truth. It means spending extra money to purchase vegetables pre-cut, beans in the can, buying a smoothie or juice or pre-made veggie burgers instead of making them at home. During times when training is intense, I will absolutely lean toward convenience in order to plate up a high vibe meal. Popping up everywhere these days are online and local meal delivery services, most of which provide vegan options if they are not already completely vegan services.

I have the luxury of working at home when I'm not teaching in the studio so I can have sweet potatoes cooking in the oven or brown rice for the week simmering on the stove while I'm on a mindfulness call with an athlete. But if we were a 9-5 family, working outside of the home and commuting, you bet your bottom dollar that a vegan meal delivery service would be a staple a few times a week. Do what you need to do to serve up and eat high vibes everyday. This cookbook is a great place to start.

Keep it Simple

Eating foods closest to their natural state is not only the most nutritious way to consume nature's abundance but is ultra efficient for people who have small windows of time. A great way to enjoy meals like this is to dump them all into one bowl. A base of brown rice or quinoa and beans will give you tons of nutrients. Add in fresh veggies and some salsa and you have a nutritional home run on your hands.

Help yourself out by cooking up a few cups of quinoa or brown rice at the beginning of the week and set yourself up for multiple easy meal preps. Buy organic whenever possible but know that it's better to eat these meals "conventional" than not at all. Hot sauce or salsa are great substitutes for fancy sauces while avocado and lemon massaged into a pile of kale creates a delicious dressing.

Don't overthink it. Eating a whole foods plant-based diet can be simple. If you open your fridge and all you have is spinach and sweet potato then celebrate because you have a high vibe meal ready to roll. Add hemp seed and nutritional yeast from your superfood stock shelf, a little olive oil and apple cider vinegar and you have a complete meal that will satiate you for hours. What's the worst that can happen? You don't like the combo or you are still hungry. Ok, well deal with that when and if it arises. Stay out of the future and drop into the moment as this is where simplicity, contentment and creativity are found.

When in Doubt, Mono Eat.

Clearly the followup to keeping it simple. There is nothing more simple than a one ingredient meal. Avocado. A pile of sauteed kale. A bushel of roasted asparagus. A grapefruit. A banana. A baked potato. Where does it say that we have to combine a series of food items, prep it and cook it in order for our bodies to be sustained? We have created these "rules" in our minds that overcomplicate what can be very simple experiences of nutrition.

There are so many benefits to mono eating. For starters, you only have to clean up one ingredient. But also mono eating optimizes digestion, avoids overeating and helps us understand how our bodies react to certain foods. I can't tell you how many times I've eaten a huge bowl of spinach for dinner and gone to bed a very happy fed girl.

This usually happens on nights when I'm exhausted so what better way to honor that than by filling myself with something that is nutrient dense, easy to digest and requires virtually no clean up so I can get to bed as early as possible? The answer: not much. Mono eat, it's the wave of the future for busy athletes.

Don't Give Anything Up

Clear and simple, diets don't work and that is because they are based on going without. They are founded on a principle of deprivation. Deprivation of calories, deprivation of things that you enjoy and for what? So you can lose weight for a temporary period of time? This whole idea of dieting is crazy, unsustainable and hardwired with self-sabotage, leaving the dieter feeling and sometimes looking worse than before they started. So unless you are literally on death's doorstep with heart disease or diabetes or cancer, I say don't give a darn thing up.

And absolutely, without a doubt, no question in my mind, start adding in more high vibe food. If you are an eggs and bacon breakfast person, precede or accompany that meal with our Pre-Workout Green Smoothie. If you are a cheeseburger (the putrefying flesh kind) and fries person, add a side of roasted asparagus with a little salt and pepper. If you are a vegan junk food junkie consider a side of quinoa with spinach* as an addition to your next plate of processed vegan food. Even harmless food can be harmful to our bodies. Remember the cooking with colors and keep it simple tips? Of course you do, you just read them.

If you want to transition your diet to eating more plant-based whole foods, start by adding in and not by giving up. In the long run, this is our most sustainable way to make change. The microbiology in our guts adjust to new foods and those little organisms will be hungry for more. Enter, cravings for kale salad and high vibes.

Chef Note: *Mix in the spinach when the quinoa is still hot so it wilts just a bit then top with nutritional yeast.*

Remove the Doubt

I can still remember training for my first Ironman on a fully vegan diet and the fear that crept in about not having enough of what I needed to get to the starting line healthy. Any measly yawn would throw me into a thought cycle about how I was tired because I wasn't getting enough iron and protein and my muscles were wasting away. Who was I, at 40 years old, a mediocre triathlete at best going fully vegan while training for an Ironman? I mean, without my calcium from my cheese addiction, I would surely break a bone going down the stairs.

Already on the yogi path at the time, I knew that indulging these thoughts of nutrient deficiency and fear were not helpful to my training or my health so I did what my wise ol' meditation teacher always reminds me to do. I removed the doubt and I did that in two ways.

1. *Knowledge is Power* - It was a combination of knowledge and listening to my body that led me to a plant-based diet so I returned my focus to those two things. I rewatched *Forks Over Knives*, I watched a video on NutritionFacts.org everyday. I followed Dr. Neal Barnard, Dr. Garth Davis, Dr. Joel Kahn and I fed my mind with the mountains of peer-reviewed scientific data that has shown the benefits of eating a whole foods plant-based diet. I backed it up with digging into the truths behind the perfectly-packaged cheese and cellophane wrapped flank steak. I followed athletes like Rich Roll, Scott Jurek and Mac Danzig. I watched their examples, I read their feeds, I witnessed their athletic accomplishments and reminded myself that I was no different from them. I constantly checked in with myself and noticed that not only did I feel lighter and more energetic than ever before (despite a yawn or two here and there, I mean I was training for an Ironman, cut me some slack), I was recovering quickly from my workouts and I was not dealing with as many niggles as I had in the past. I constantly removed the doubt by feeding my mind with knowledge about the benefits of a plant-based diet and by paying attention on purpose to the truth of how I felt and not the wild commentary in my head. From the knowledge I gained, I knew that I could never go back and frankly when it all came down to it, I was feeling pretty dang good.

2. *Blood Work* - Just like the amazing tool called Google that can help us get information about the world, there is another amazing tool called a blood draw that gives us a chance to see what is happening on the inside of our bodies. I'm not talking about the chintzy data that is covered by insurance, I'm talking about extensive blood work that will reveal iron levels, cortisol, B-12, calcium, Vitamin D and yes.....protein! Services like Inside Tracker provide this type of data plus easy-to-read results with accompanying resources and explanations. Since becoming fully vegan in 2011, I have had my blood tested twice. My first blood draw was one year after shifting my diet and although I was not deficient in any particular category, we deduced that my results showed that I was not absorbing my nutrients as well as I could have been. I made some shifts in food combining, simplified my meals and applied mindful eating techniques to aid in my digestion. Since then, I have continued to feel even better and younger even as I age. The next round of blood work I received was in 2017 and I'm excited to say that not only am I in the normal, healthy range for all nutrients and levels but I am in the optimal range for most. I have since completed three Ironman distance triathlons and many other races including an ultramarathon since becoming 100% plant-based. My recovery is quick, my energy remains high and most of all, my heart is healed because I am no longer contributing to the harmful effects of animal laden nutrition.

PLANT-BASED BASICS

Stock your home with the staples of high vibe eating. This is the perfect way to limit poor food choices and the following list will give you a major jump start. At any given time this is what you will find in our cabinets and fridge. I can see dozens of meals within this list, easy to prepare and easy to find.

Produce

- Kale
- Spianch
- Peppers
- Zucchini/Squash*
- Broccoli/Cauliflower*
- Potato/Yam

Fruit

- Banana
- Grapefruit/Orange/Apple/Melon*
- Berries
- Avocado
- Lemon
- Lime

Bulk

- Brown Rice
- Quinoa
- Lentils - green/red/yellow*
- Nuts/Seeds*
- Raisins
- Nutritional Yeast
- Oats - rolled/steel cut
- Beans - Pinto/Black/Garbanzo*

Spices

- Cinnamon
- Turmeric
- Coriander
- Cumin
- Cayenne Pepper
- Curry
- Basil
- Oregano
- Paprika

Additional

- Nut Butter - peanut/almond/cashew*
- Tempeh/Tofu*
- Veggie Burgers
- Oil - coconut/olive*
- Apple Cider Vinegar
- Bragg's Liquid Aminos
- Hummus
- Salsa
- Tortilla/Wraps
- Sprouted Grain Bread
- Tortilla chips - because we all have to get our crunch on!
- Superfoods** - hemp/chia seed, goji berries, cacao nibs/powder, maca, moringa, acai
- Ground flaxseed/applesauce (make great egg substitutes)
- Hot sauce
- Coconut milk (in the can)
- Protein Powder (plant-based of course, we use Garden of Life RAW)

Chef Note:

Rotate through a variety of these items, don't feel that you have to have them all on hand. Build your supplies over time.

**Superfoods are a super easy way to boost the nutrition of any meals but they can definitely break the bank. Although we are big supporters of local businesses and farmer's markets we are not shy about getting our pricey items from larger online retailers. These are great ways to save money while getting the benefits of on-hand super items like chia and hemp seeds, goji berries, cacao nibs and powders like moringa, maca and acai. Another great option is to buy them bulk and just get what you need.*

MINDFUL EATING

Here's how it usually goes down for me at my home office. Perhaps this scenario sounds familiar? I get stumped, vexed, frustrated, bored (fill in your own adjective here) with the task at hand or just need a break for no particular reason. The next thing I know, I'm in the kitchen with a handful of tortilla chips and I'm munching away. I lose count as I stand looking into the fridge deliberating about what I want to eat. This lasts until I end up grabbing the salsa only to hammer down more chips. I could go on with this story but I think we know how it ends, right?

The kale goes unopened, the roof of my mouth is sore from being jabbed with tortilla corners, I get tired in 20 minutes and I'm hungry again in 30. I understand that tortilla chips and salsa, especially the GMO-free, organic kind that I stock in the house, don't equal worst-case scenario but the food here really isn't the issue. It's the mindlessness in which I put food into my body that causes my distress, GI or otherwise.

So now that we're out in the open about mindless eating and you know that I'm not some priestess up on her high horse (at least not in this life), let's talk about mindful eating.

Mindfulness, which is the basis of mindful eating, comes from the Buddhist practice of being aware of what is happening within and around you at the moment. When applied to eating, it can take on many different forms. From chewing your food many times to noticing the color, texture, temperature and taste of each bite. It can mean getting rid of distractions like eating while watching television or even reading a book. Essentially my translation of this practice means to slow down and just do one thing, eat. And within this, insert food, chew food, swallow food before you put another bite in and repeat, one step at a time.

How does mindful eating help in transitioning to a plant-based diet?

Mindful eating practices give us the opportunity to notice our food choices and also gives us the chance to deal with anxiety and other feelings like guilt around food. It shines a light on our relationship to food which for many is emotional and a breeding ground for attachment (i.e. I could never live with my meat/cheese/cereal/Pop Tarts and yes even kale, we can form attachments to healthy food too). Food is fuel, nothing more, and mindful eating makes room to discover this concept of neutrality.

Mindfulness is being aware of a moment while it is unfolding without judgement and this is the essence of neutrality. It slows us down enough where we don't miss the experience of eating and we are present to notice how the food feels once it is in our bodies. The slowing down aspect of mindful eating makes a space between wanting the food and eating the food.

In other words if the food on the end of your fork is not aligned with your commitment and goal, you will find yourself in a gap where you can make another choice. The more we choose away from the conditioned behaviors and out-of-date belief systems, the wider the neural pathways become for our new behaviors and belief systems about how we fuel our bodies and what it takes to make that happen (meal prep, cooking at home).

How does mindful eating help with performance?

Besides bringing consciousness to the food that we're putting in our bodies, mindful eating requires us to slow down and chew our food. The saying, while I'm not sure of its origin, "chew your liquids and drink your solids" are wise words to live by.

When we slow down and chew our food thoroughly before swallowing, our bodies are able to break down the food more efficiently. Digestion begins in the mouth and if we are shoveling food in, swallowing before it's properly chewed because we're already onto the next spoonful, then the oral digestion phase is heavily compromised. But when we do slow down and chew our food, especially plant foods, less energy is required on behalf of our bodies to break down our meal, leaving more energy for training.

Our digestive system is governed by our Parasympathetic Nervous System which directs blood flow to the digestive tract, stimulates the salivary glands and increases peristalsis, all of which allow for better absorption of nutrients and breakdown of food. So when we are rushed or stressed, our digestion suffers.

When we eat mindfully, the simple act of this practice slows us down, stimulates our healing nervous system and allows our digestive tract to work to its fullest potential. Pulling more nutrition out of our food will create less battle in our bellies (and minds) and lead to a healthier body (and mind). A healthier body and mind leads to better performance. Mindful eating will also lower your chances of over or under eating, leading to your ideal weight for performance.

Simple Mindful Eating Practices

To bring more mindfulness to your eating habits try one of these tips consistently during two meals per week. If you dive in and try to do all five with every meal you are setting yourself up for unsustainable change. Just add in slowly and notice the subtle changes in your relationship to the ritual of eating.

Master one of these practices before adding in more, stay focused:

1) Consider your food before your start eating it. Notice the color, texture, taste. Contemplate how it got to your plate: harvesting, travel, the package, and the people involved in its journey.

2) When you eat, just eat. No television, no technology, no reading, no conversation, no music.

3) Use your non-dominant hand to eat.

4) Put your fork down between each bite.

5) Set your timer for 20 minutes and use all that time to eat your meal.

SMOOTHIES AND DRINKS

PRE-WORKOUT GREEN SMOOTHIE

This blend makes a 24 ounce smoothie. If we use it as a pre-run shake or pre-yoga, then we'll drink it about 2-3 hours before especially if we're using peanut butter, since it is more oily than almond butter. This is a great option if you are a 9-5'er to have around 3pm prior to your after-work training session or if you're just a pb junkie like BJ and want to surround your addiction with spinach.

Prep Time: 5 minutes
Cook Time: zero
Servings: 1-2

Ingredients:

1 apple

1 banana, ripe

1 cup spinach

1 tablespoon of nut butter (almond, peanut or whatever you have)

1 cup almond milk, unsweetened

4-6 cubes ice

Preparation:

1. Combine all ingredients in a high-powered blender.
2. Blend until smooth and creamy and enjoy! See, eating healthy doesn't have to be difficult. Blend and drink. You got this.

JUMPSTART ELIXER

If I had a dime for every time I fought the urge to grab coffee before this drink, I wouldn't need to sell a cookbook to make rent (please people, I didn't write this book to pay my rent, I wrote it to create a better world, but thank you for making the purchase). Seriously, this is the best part of my day and the most challenging. It's like meditation, my mind has so many readily-available excuses as to why I don't need this and so many readily-available counterarguments to drink up, like boosting metabolism, aiding digestion, flushing out toxins and getting a headstart on hydration.

Take it from a girl with experience, this Jumpstart Elixir is exactly what you want in your body before anything else touches your insides. It has a knack for aiding in getting what's in you, out of you (if you know what I mean). After this, coffee away my friends, coffee away!

Prep Time: 2-20 minutes depending on grogginess
Cook Time: zero
Servings: 1

Ingredients:
16 ounces of warm filtered water
Juice of ¼ lemon
⅛ teaspoon cayenne pepper

Preparation:
1. Combine all ingredients together and stir.
2. Continue to stir as you drink to keep cayenne from settling at the bottom unless you really need a good ole' kick in the butt, athlete's choice.

WATERMELON COOLER

We are all individual and therefore our needs are unique to us. Never more so is this evident than with the people you spend the most time with....ahem, BJ. One of the things I've come to learn about BJ is that he's not always ready to eat immediately after a training session, especially when they are intense, especially when it is hot. So I've found this to be the perfect post-workout potion that is easy on his belly while jumpstarting recovery until he's ready for a meal. The coconut water and watermelon are uber hydrating and will help with replenishment of glycogen stores and electrolyte balance. Lime is a proven digestive aid and the basil is rich in antioxidants which can help with soft tissue repair and post-workout inflammation.

Prep Time: 7 minutes

Cook Time: zero

Servings: 1-2 depending on your thirst factor

Ingredients:

2 cups watermelon

1.5 cups coconut water

Juice of 1 lime

5 basil leaves

Ice

Preparation:

1. Combine all ingredients in a blender for 1 minute.
2. Pour over ice and serve.
3. If you're in a fancy pants mood or you have sweaty workout pals over at your house that you want to impress, add a straw and garnish with lime. Take that, fancy pants!

CINNAMON ALMOND SMOOTHIE

We love, love cinnamon almonds and we've been guilty of eating ourselves into "nut gut" more than a few times. BJ even solicited our friend Tara to send his favorite brand across the country just to satisfy his craving - now that's serious cinnamon almond microbiome!

This smoothie is that same tasty treat in a drinkable form with an added superfood twist. I love this blend as a meal replacer or when I'm just not in the mood to chop up kale and especially when I'm on the run. It's a hefty blend so drink it at least 2-3 hours before a workout to allow time for your body to absorb its satiating goodness.

Prep Time: 7 minutes

Cook Time: zero

Servings: 16 ounce smoothie

Ingredients:

1 banana, ripe

1 cup almond milk, unsweetened

1 tablespoon almond butter

2 pitted medjool dates

2 teaspoons cinnamon

1 tablespoon chia seeds

1 tablespoon hemp seeds

1 scoop of Vanilla Protein Powder (we like Garden of Life Raw brand)

4 whole walnuts

Preparation:

1. Combine all ingredients in a high powered blender.
2. Blend and pour into your favorite glass and enjoy.

Chef Note: *Options to sprinkle on top: cacao nibs, nut butter drizzle and of course, extra cinnamon - hello regulated blood sugar!*

RECOVERY SMOOTHIE

Here it is, our go-to that we've turned to too many times to count at this point. We find that the triathlon life requires a hefty dose of low ingredient, low step, I can make it in my sleep type of recipes and this is one of those. It's power-packed and perfect for a post-workout fuel up. Pineapple is ideal for recovery because it contains the enzyme Bromelain which aids in the digestion of protein and may also aid in the reduction of inflammation. Spinach has been shown to help build muscle by speeding up the conversion of protein to muscle, not to mention, it's packed with iron and calcium while tropical fruit, like pineapple aid in the absorption of nonheme iron found in plants. Bananas are packed with potassium which plays a key role in muscle energy and this is a nutrient that can be zapped during training sessions. Need I go on?

Ok fine. The plant-based protein speaks for itself as well as the non-dairy almond milk avoiding the inflammatory response that dairy from an animal will elicit in the body. Honestly, in a nutshell (lame pun intended) this is a full body restorative blend that tastes dang good! We use frozen fruit and veggies because it removes the ice factor and since they are flash frozen they tend to have higher nutrient values than "fresh produce" that has traveled from far away.

Prep Time: 7 minutes

Cook Time: zero

Servings: 1

Ingredients:

½ cup pineapple, chopped

1 banana, ripe

1 ½ cups spinach

1 scoop vanilla plant-based protein powder (we like Garden of Life Raw brand)

1 cup almond milk, unsweetened

Preparation:

1. Combine all ingredients in a high-powered blender.
2. Blend until creamy and smooth.

Chef Note: Up the vibe with toppings like goji berries and cacao nibs. For an extra anti-inflammatory punch add up to 2 teaspoons of turmeric and a dash of black pepper. BJ is not a fan of this addition however, I LOVE what it offers in this blend.

BREAKFAST

CINNAMON BREAKFAST BAKE

Please, if you do anything in this life, break the office donut cycle and do it with this delish breakfast bake. You will be a hero of modern times! Perfect for breakfast, an afternoon sweet or nightly dessert. Or be like BJ, snack monster extraordinaire, and eat this right out of the pan every time you pass it by. No plate or utensil necessary. This dish was inspired by a bake I saw on the website Meaningful Eats. I took creative liberty to make it 100% plant-based and cruelty-free while adding a touch of superfood love.

Prep Time: 20 minutes

Cook Time: 25 minutes

Servings: 6-8 hungry vegans

Ingredients:

3 tablespoons of filtered water

1 tablespoon flaxseed, ground

1 cup uncooked quinoa, rinsed

2 cups filtered water

¾ cup pureed extra firm tofu (½ of 14-ounce container)

1 tablespoon chia seed

⅓ cup non-dairy milk, unsweetened but sometimes I used vanilla for extra flavor

⅓ cup maple syrup

1 tablespoon cinnamon

1 teaspoon vanilla extract

Sweet Cashew Cream (recipe on page 84)

Preparation:

1. Preheat the oven to 375°F.
2. Combine 3 tablespoons of water and 1 tablespoon of ground flaxseed. Set aside for 15 minutes.
3. Bring water to boil, add quinoa, stir to combine, turn to medium-low. Cover and cook for 15 minutes or until most of the water has been absorbed. Remove from heat and allow to cool completely.

Continued on next page

Preparation:

4. Line an 8-by-8-inch baking pan with lightly greased parchment and set aside. A cake pan will also do the trick and I've been known to bake this in my deep skillet.

5. Puree tofu in a food processor or high-powered blender until smooth.*

6. Combine smooth tofu, ground flaxseed-water mixture, non-dairy milk, maple syrup, vanilla extract and cinnamon in a mixing bowl.

7. Add cooled quinoa and mix thoroughly.

8. Add chia seed, mix.

9. Pour into the parchment-lined baking dish and spread it around to ensure that it's even.

10. Top with a sprinkle of cinnamon.

11. Bake for 25 to 30 minutes until set and golden.

12. Using parchment, remove bake immediately and set on cooling grate.

13. Serve with fresh fruit & berries and sweet cashew cream or with a dollop of nut butter or all of it together!

Chef Note: Prep and cool the quinoa ahead of time and save time here. Plus getting into the habit of having whole grains and high power seeds like quinoa on hand is a plus to your plant-based success.

*Don't have a high-powered blender or food processor? Don't sweat it..whisk or mash tofu until smooth.

CHUNKY MONKEY MORNING TOAST

Watch out, this morning toast packs a punch. For me, this leaves my belly satiated for hours although I've been known to go back for a second piece especially in the thick of Ironman training. Sometimes I have success with this decision and other times I am left to navigate the aftermath of overeating (exit training, enter nap). This toast is so delicious that the real mission here is to eat it mindfully, chew each bite in it's entirety, take time in between bites to bring your awareness to the moment or the mindful eating section of this book.

Prep Time: 5 minutes

Cook Time: 5 minutes

Servings: 1

Ingredients:

1 piece of sprouted grain bread (we like Ezekiel brand)

1 teaspoon Agave or maple syrup

1-2 tablespoons crunchy peanut butter (oh yeah!)

1 teaspoon chia seed

1/2 banana, ripe and chopped

1 teaspoon chia seed

1 tablespoon shredded coconut or coconut flakes, unsweetened

Preparation:

1. Toast bread to your liking then drizzle with agave.
2. Next, spread peanut butter, sprinkle chia seeds, then top with banana slices and coconut.
3. Press the coconut into the banana to avoid excess run-off.
4. Licking the plate is allowed and encouraged if anything is left on it after you devour this Aloha inspired meal.

WHAT THE KALE? OATMEAL

Raisins, walnuts, berries in my oatmeal? Sure. Of course. Kale? Not so sure? Give it a shot people, keep all channels open! Trust this high-viber to start your day. The way the kale is cooked in with the oatmeal blends it in perfectly. The combination of tastes gives this morning porridge some major POW! And as athletes isn't more POW exactly what we're trying to attain? Our performance starts with what we put into our body so start here. POW!

Prep Time: 5 minutes

Cook Time: 10 minutes

Servings: 2

Ingredients:

1 ¾ cup filtered water

1 cup rolled oats (gluten-free is an option, just not quick oats)

1 ½ cups kale, chopped small

½ cup golden raisins (or whatever you have)

6 Brazil nuts, chopped

2 teaspoons hemp seeds

1 teaspoon cinnamon

1 teaspoon agave nectar

½ cup sliced strawberries

1 tablespoon almond butter (who are we kidding...who can stop with just 1 tablespoon?!)

Preparation:

1. Bring water to a boil, add oats return to boil then turn down to med - med/low and cover partially (leave a little room for air to escape, this avoids the classic oatmeal boil over). Cook 5-7 minutes.
2. When it is still a bit watery, add raisins and kale, turn to low. Cook 2 minutes covered, until kale softens and turns vibrant green (super yum).
3. Stir in cinnamon, brazil nuts and agave.
4. Serve up, top with strawberries, hemp seeds and almond butter - oh my and enjoy!

TOFU SCRAMBLE

The perfect transition dish for egg lovers looking for more plant-based options. BJ was a major "egg man". He would scramble upwards of 8-10 a day just for him because he truly believed that he needed all that protein (silly man!). He was reluctant to buy into my tofu scramble but eventually he gave it a try, and like a child who hates broccoli but tries broccoli, he balanced the tiniest piece of tofu, almost invisible to the naked eye, on the edge of his fork. He popped it in and quickly decided that it wasn't that bad. Well that teeny weeny piece of tofu has now turned into requests for more and more and more. This is not just breakfast in our house, many times we have it for lunch and dinner. For those in transition, the turmeric not only offers intense anti-inflammatory agents but this potent spice even makes this dish look like scrambled eggs. Score one for mind trickery!

Prep time: 10 minutes

Cook time: 10 minutes

Servings: 2

Ingredients:

1 teaspoon coconut oil

½ 14-ounce container of firm or extra firm tofu, drained

½ -1 teaspoon turmeric* (can add bitter taste so if you don't love turmeric go light)

½ teaspoon cumin

1 cup red pepper, diced (about 1 medium size pepper)

1 cup zucchini, diced

1 cup chopped broccoli (about 1 small crown)

1-2 cups kale (6-7 kale leaves depending on size)

½ cup chickpeas, rinsed and drained

Suggested Toppings:

Avocado

Hemp Seeds

Nutritional Yeast

Hot sauce or salsa

Fresh chopped tomatoes

Salt and fresh ground black pepper to taste

Continued on next page

TOFU SCRAMBLE

Preparation:

1. In a medium size skillet or saute pan on medium, heat up the coconut oil.

2. Once pan is warm, saute crumbled tofu for 2-3 minutes.

3. Next, add turmeric and cumin, mix together.

4. Add chopped veggies and chickpeas.

5. Saute 5-7 minutes, add greens in the final minute or so to soften.

6. Top with avocado slices, hemp seeds, nutritional yeast, salsa or hot sauce.

Chef Note: *After an especially big workout, we'll also add a piece of sprouted grain toast with nut butter. And for dessert, we highly recommend a short walk and a long nap.*

SALADS

ROOT DOWN SALAD

My friends chatted about how to make beets taste good on a sleepy ride home from yoga training one night. Fighting to stay awake I remembered tidbits of cayenne and carrots. I find beets to be a very intense vegetable but this recipe perfectly neutralizes the sweetness of the beets leaving just great texture and taste. Serve up for lunch on a bed of greens and topped with chickpeas. The morning after that sleepy ride home I created this salad and yes it requires some prep but with no cooking time I still think it's a win. Except for when BJ makes it and I spend the rest of my day spotting beet stains all over the kitchen. How it is that he can get it on the ceiling?

Prep Time: 15 minutes

Cook Time: zero

Servings: 4-6

Ingredients:

3 cups of raw beets, shredded

3 cups of carrots, shredded

6 radish, shredded

1 lime, zest and juice (about ¼ cup)*

2 tablespoons apple cider vinegar

2 tablespoons olive oil (optional)

3 teaspoons cumin

¼ teaspoon cayenne pepper (optional-more or less, depending how much heat you prefer)

Preparation:

1. Combine beets, carrots and radishes in a medium size mixing bowl.
2. Zest lime and squeeze in the fresh lime juice.
3. Add apple cider vinegar and olive oil, if using.
4. Add spices cumin and cayenne pepper.
5. Mix well and allow flavors to come together before serving, at least 30 minutes to an hour.
6. Season with fresh ground black pepper and salt optional.

SIMPLY KALE SALAD

This salad is pretty much my everyday go-to for lunch. It guarantees that I'm getting my daily dose of dark leafies and I'm left feeling energetic. There's no three o'clock nosedive with this mean green dish, you can count on its high vibration to keep you going.

The recipe below is the quantity that I make for BJ and I because we like really big salads but I think it could be served as a side salad for up to four people. I have to warn you, it is addicting and one person eating an entire bushel of kale with this recipe is not unheard of. Quantities may differ depending on the girth of your kale so always make to your taste preferences. This is an easily adjustable recipe and pretty darn difficult to screw up.

Prep Time: 10 minutes
Cook Time: zero
Servings: 2-4

Ingredients:
1 bunch of kale, chopped or torn (about 6-8 leaves depending on size)
2 tablespoons olive oil (optional)
1 tablespoon apple cider vinegar (depending on your taste buds)
¼ cup nutritional yeast
¼ cup hemp seeds
⅛ cup flaxseed, ground
¼ cup of dried cranberries
Salt and fresh ground cracked pepper (optional)

Preparation:
1. Wash kale, tear leaves off their stalk and into bite size pieces.
2. Add olive oil and vinegar.
3. Massage kale until soft, the color should deepen. Get into it, feel the plant and get connected to your food.
4. Toss in nutritional yeast, hemp seeds, ground flaxseed and cranberries.
5. Season with salt and fresh ground cracked pepper. (optional)
6. Serve with extra nutritional yeast on the side if you're a "nooch" junkie like me and enjoy.

POWER PACKED QUINOA SALAD

When BJ and I are in the throws of training, having a salad like this on hand is more than a godsend. Truly, it feels like a miracle meal. I usually whip up a batch of this and freeze half for our next build phase when our bodies are shelled and hungry all the time. Having a meal on hand where all you have to do is take it out of the freezer in the morning makes for a happy and hungerless home.

This meal has everything you need so don't shy away from making it your one bowl lunch or dinner. It also serves as a great side dish and the quantity of this recipe is enough so that you can bring to a party and wow all your friends with your high vibe side. "Yes it is vegan, yes it tastes really good!", be prepared to say this about one million times.

Prep Time: 20 minutes
Cook Time: 15 minutes
Servings: 8-10

Ingredients:

1 cup organic sweet yellow corn (frozen is easiest)

1/2 cup uncooked/rinsed organic quinoa (approximately 2 cups cooked)

4 cups of filtered water

1 12oz bag frozen organic edamame shelled

¼ cup chopped organic red onion

1 cup chopped organic cilantro

1 can organic black beans drained/rinsed

1/4 cup organic sprouts (alfalfa, broccoli, pea, sunflower, any type of sprout will suffice)

1/4 cup shredded organic red cabbage

2 tablespoon olive oil

juice of fresh lime

1/2 cup unsalted organic sunflower seeds

2 teaspoons salt (optional)

Fresh ground black pepper (optional)

Continued on next page

POWER PACKED QUINOA SALAD

Preparation:

1. Add frozen corn to large mixing bowl and let it sit at room temperature to help with defrosting.

2. Bring 1 cup water to boil, add quinoa, stir to combine, turn to medium-low. Cover and cook for 15 minutes or until most of the water has been absorbed. When quinoa is done, fluff with fork and combine with corn as this will help to complete the defrost.

3. In a medium saucepan, bring 3 cups of water to a boil and add edamame. Cook on medium-high heat for 3-5 minutes. When cooked, add to quinoa and corn mixture.

4. While the edamame is cooking, you can prep the other raw ingredients. And add into the corn bowl at any time.

5. Combine onion, cilantro, black beans, sprouts, red cabbage, edamame to quinoa/corn mixture.

6. Add olive oil, lime and sunflower seeds, stir to combine.

7. Season with salt and fresh ground black pepper.

8. Serve as a meal or side dish or straight out of the mixing bowl. I'm all in for minimal clean up.

REFRESHINGLY SIMPLE SPINACH SALAD

This high-vibe pile of plants is perfectly light to serve as a complement to any meal or cut the servings in half and have a big ole' portion for yourself as your meal. Despite it's light nature it still manages to move the power meter a few notches. Healthy fats from the walnuts will give a nice dose of omega-3, while the Vitamin C will aid in the absorption of iron from the spinach and the chia seeds will give us all a ride on the protein superfood bus. Takeaway: never underestimate the power of plants.

Prep Time: 7 minutes

Cook Time: zero

Servings: 2-4

Ingredients:

2 cups spinach (or any green you prefer)

1 cup strawberries, sliced

½ cup dried cranberries

¼ cup red onion, thinly sliced

2 tablespoons walnuts, roughly chopped

1 tablespoon chia seeds

Citrus balsamic dressing (recipe on page 81)

Preparation:

1. Combine all salad ingredients in a mixing bowl.
2. Combine balsamic dressing ingredients in small bowl, whisk together.
3. Pour dressing over salad and gently toss.
4. Plate up as one serving for lunch or two servings as a side dish.

Chef Note: *You know what would be amazing as an add-on to this salad? An artisan plant-based soft cheese. In supermarkets, we love Miyokos, Tree Line and Kite Hill but maybe you are lucky enough to live near a vegan cheese shop. For sure they are delicacies, but they are well worth the cost if you're in the mood for turning a superfood bus into a magic carpet ride.*

ENTREES

SUN-DRIED TOMATO TEMPEH PIZZA

This creation was the product of realizing I had no olive oil in the house to make pesto and no spinach, which is a major foundation of most of my pizzas. Being my biggest counter side cheerleader, BJ held out hope. I was exhausted and seriously craving pizza (hello pizza microbiome!). I was looking left, right, up and down for shortcuts to get a homemade pizza into our bellies post haste and this was the end result. This pie is the perfect example of what a high vibe kitchen can turn out when it appears that there is nothing to eat. Secretly, those are my favorite experiences of creation.

Prep Time: 15 minutes
Cook Time: 20 minutes
Servings: How hungry are you?

Ingredients:

1 bunch of asparagus (sliced into 1 inch segments)

1 tablespoon coconut oil OR olive oil (this can be made without oil)

1 8-ounce package of organic tempeh (not a tempeh fan, mushrooms would also work well)

1 cup of sliced sun-dried tomatoes (dried OR packed in olive oil*)

1 10-inch pre-made pizza crust (our favorite is Whole Foods brand-cook at home)

¼ cup hummus (lemon or original)*

2 cups basil leaves, rough chopped or gently torn

1 cup vegan mozzarella cheese (we prefer Follow Your Heart brand)

¼ cup hemp seeds

Preparation:

1. Preheat oven to 450 degrees with a pizza stone. (No pizza stone, no problem. Cookie sheet works well too.)
2. On a small cookie sheet roast asparagus (dry, no oil) for about 6-10 minutes depending on thickness. You don't want to cook it all the way through because it will continue to cook on the pizza. Once done, remove from oven and set aside to cool.
3. While asparagus is cooking, prepare the tempeh. Cut tempeh block into 1-inch thick slices. In a medium saute pan, warm 1 tablespoon of olive oil (if using) on medium heat. Add the tempeh when the pan is hot and cook until well done, about 8-10 minutes.
4. Once tempeh is sufficiently browned, remove from heat and break it up using a wooden spoon or spatula. It will result in messy cuts and crumbles-perfect as pizza toppings. Yum!

Continued on next page

SUN-DRIED TOMATO TEMPEH PIZZA

Preparation:

5. Add in the sun-dried tomatoes and asparagus to the tempeh mixture and stir to combine.

6. If cooking your own crust remove from oven after following directions of the dough purchased. If using pre-packaged, then remove hot stone from oven and place crust on top.

7. Assemble the pizza. Using the hummus as pizza sauce, smear on a good base layer. If the crust is hot out of the oven the hummus may soak in a bit so use more to ensure that saucy taste, maybe another 3 table-spoons or so.

8. Next add tempeh-veggie mixture.

9. Finally top with fresh basil leaves, hemp seeds and vegan mozzarella cheese.

Bake in the oven for 8-10 minutes or until golden brown. Allow to cool slightly before cutting and enjoy with friends. It's pizza night, bring on the joy!

Chef Note: *Sun-dried tomatoes add a punch of tomato flavor not to mention a rocking source of Vitamin C, K, Iron and the kick butt antioxidant lycopene which can lower risk of certain cancers. We recommend a small jar of them packed in pure olive oil to use in this recipe because it will give your tempeh/veggie mixture some moisture and flavor. If you prefer dried tomatoes-and no oil, just soak them in a small bowl of filtered water for 5-10 minutes to soften them up and rehydrate them for this amazing pizza (throw a tablespoon or two of hummus into the tempeh/veggie mixture so it's not too dry).*

BUDDHA BOWL WITH AVOCADO TAHINI SAUCE

This meal can be prepared in a matter of minutes if you prep quinoa and sweet potato ahead of time. And while you're at it, prep more than one potato and more than 1 cup of quinoa. These high vibe extras can serve as the foundation of other meals throughout the week. There really isn't much to prep here, just a few minutes to slice up the potatoes and heat the beans, unless of course you choose to soak and cook your beans and in that case, definitely cook those ahead of time. This is such a spot-on, super easy vegan dinner party meal. Start things off with some plant-based artisan cheese, flatbread and fruit then end with small Coconut Banana Bread sandwiches with the Cacao Hazelnut spread in the middle (and thick). Throw in some Kombucha and call it a night people because you nailed it!

Prep Time: 10 minutes
Cook Time: 45-50 minutes (depending on the size of sweet potatoes)
Servings: 2-4

Ingredients:

2-4 sweet potatoes (approximately ½ - full sweet potato per person depending on size)

1 cup uncooked quinoa, rinsed

1 15-ounce can of black beans OR 2 cups of black beans

1 cup fresh cilantro, chopped

2 tablespoons hemp seed

2 tablespoons pumpkin seeds

Avocado Tahini Sauce (recipe on page 85)

Preparation:

1. Preheat oven to 400 degrees.
2. Wash and poke sweet potatoes several times with a fork (this will help them cook faster) OR cut sweet potatoes into small cubes and bake on a small cookie sheet. Bake potatoes for 30-40 minutes depending on their size. They should be fork tender when done.
3. While potatoes are cooking start to prepare your quinoa. In a small to medium saucepan bring 2 cups of water to a boil. Once boiling, add the quinoa, stir to combine, cover and let cook for 13-15 minutes. Allow to rest off the heat, covered for 10 minutes. Then fluff quinoa with a fork and set aside.

Continued on next page

BUDDHA BOWL WITH AVOCADO TAHINI SAUCE

Preparation:

4. In another pan, heat beans on stove in their liquid (if using canned)* over medium heat until they start to bubble then reduce heat to low while the sweet potatoes finish cooking.

5. Prepare your cilantro. Chop and set aside. Once potatoes are cooked and cool enough to handle, chop them into small cubes.

6. To assemble your bowl: Layer items anyway you like. It does not have to Instagram worthy! Quinoa, potatoes, black beans, cilantro, avocado tahini sauce, pumpkin seeds, hemp seeds.

Chef Note: *If you've already cooked your beans from scratch and they are chillin' in the fridge waiting to nourish your body, reheat on the stove using 2 cups of filtered water. (Truth be told, I skip heating the beans all the time, no biggie).*

IRON MAIDEN

Where do you get your protein? Calcium? Iron? Ummmm, this meal. This dish is packed with all of the above and includes high vibe healing spices like curry, cumin and turmeric. This is one of our weekly staples during the height of training and it's even better the next day over a bed of fresh spinach. Serve with warm vegan naan bread for an over the top weeknight meal. And feel free to add sliced avocado and hot sauce for those who like it creamy and spicy. Oooolala!

Prep Time: 5 minutes
Cook Time: 20 minutes
Servings: 4-6

Ingredients:
5 cups of filtered water
1 cup green lentils, dry
1 cup red lentils, dry
1 14-ounce can of coconut milk, divided
1 tablespoon turmeric
1 tablespoon curry
2 teaspoons cumin
½ teaspoon cayenne (start with a ¼ teaspoon if you don't like the heat)
1 cup tomatoes, chopped and seeded OR 1 14-ounce can of diced tomatoes
3 cups broccoli, chopped small
½ cup cashews, rough chopped
2-3 cups spinach, rough chopped (about 2 large handfuls)
½ teaspoon sea or himalayan salt (optional)
Fresh ground black pepper to taste (optional)
Hot sauce (optional, we like Cholula brand)

Preparation:
1. In a medium saucepan bring 3 cups of water to a boil. Once boiling, add the green lentils, stir to combine, turn to medium-low heat, cover and cook for 15-20 minutes.
2. Meanwhile, in a deep or large skillet, bring 2 cups of water and 1 cup of the coconut milk to a boil. Add in the red lentils, stir to combine, reduce heat to medium-low. Cover and cook for 10-12 minutes. Lentils should be firm, starting to get soft, but not too mushy.

Continued on next page

IRON MAIDEN

Preparation:

3. Then add in all the spices to the red lentil mixture and stir to combine. Allow to cook for about 2 minutes, then add tomatoes and cook for another 3-5 minutes.

4. Next add in the rest of the can of coconut milk (about ½ cup), cashews and chopped broccoli to red lentil mixture. Stir to combine and continue to cook for another 3-5 minutes.

5. Drain green lentils* and add just 2 cups to the red lentil mixture and stir to combine. Then add chopped spinach cover and cook for another 2-3 minutes until spinach starts to wilt.

6. Season with salt and fresh ground black pepper to taste.

7. Serve in a bowl and top with hot sauce for those of you who want a little extra heat. Also excellent served on a bed of warm rice or more greens.

Chef Note: The rest of the green lentils can be added on top of green salads or frozen to be used in another recipe. This dish is excellent to serve to a crowd.

JACKFRUIT TACOS WITH CHIPOTLE SAUCE

When I was a kid, I always had the same two top picks for birthday meals. 1) Tacos 2) Double thick Shake n' Bake pork chops. One of those picks still ranks top on my list of favorite meals. The other, I'm thankful to say, is not even on my radar. But if you are a current or recovering fan of pulled pork, these tacos will surely give you the fix you need while not harming the planet or any of our animal friends. We are fortunate to have fresh jackfruit here in Southern California but I always keep a case of canned in my cabinets that I buy online.

Prep Time: 10 minutes
Cook Time: 10 minutes
Yield: 6-8 tacos

Ingredients:

1 15-ounce can of black beans, rinsed and drained

2 teaspoons paprika, divided

1 teaspoon chili powder

1 clove garlic, minced

¼ cup of filtered water

1 14-ounce can of jackfruit OR 2 cups fresh (for canned we like Native Forest)

½ cup barbecue sauce (pick your favorite, we like Amy's brand because it seems to be sold in all major grocery stores)

2 teaspoons cumin

Taco Toppings:

1 cup purple cabbage, chopped or grated thin

¼ cup scallions, finely chopped

½ cup cilantro, rough chopped

1-2 limes, cut into wedges

1 package of corn OR whole grain tortillas OR taco shells

Almond Chipotle Sauce (recipe on page 86)

Continued on next page

JACKFRUIT TACOS WITH CHIPOTLE SAUCE

Preparation:

1. Preheat your oven to 200 degrees.

2. In a medium saucepan add black beans, chili powder and 1 teaspoon of paprika on medium heat. Bring mixture to slow boil, reduce heat to low and allow to simmer, stirring occasionally.

3. Meanwhile in another pan, place garlic and water and cook on medium-low for about 3-5 minutes, or until garlic is fragrant. Watch this closely-garlic will burn quickly and it becomes very bitter. Add more water if needed.

4. Next prepare the jackfruit. If using canned, rinse and drain. Rough chop or use your hands to break apart into small shreds. Add jackfruit, barbeque sauce and spices to the pan, stir to combine. Simmer jackfruit mixture for 5-10 minutes or until heated through, stirring occasionally.

5. While the jackfruit and beans are simmering, prepare your taco topping and tortillas. Chop or grate cabbage and thinly slice green onions, pull the leaves from the cilantro stalks, cut lime wedges and set aside. Feel free to get creative here and add in what you have on hand or what your prefer. Anything goes for taco night.

6. Heat tortillas in the oven until warm, about 2-4 minutes or heat for 10-20 seconds in the microwave. Serve tacos family style and let everyone build their own plate. Enjoy with a side of black beans with a fresh sprig of cilantro, almond chipotle sauce and lime wedges.

ROASTED VEGETABLE PASTA WITH HEMP SEED PESTO

Please! This cookbook is for athletes. Did you really think I wasn't going to include a pasta dish? Even though we may all try and hide it, let's just come clean and admit that we all love and crave indulgent carbs like pasta. No shame with this high vibe linguine as the addition of roasted veggies and hemp seed pesto bumps up the nutritional content of a traditional pasta and sauce meal. We've found great success in the past few years with using gluten-free pasta, oh how far we've come! Although gluten doesn't seem to bother BJ and I too much we have learned that it creates an inflammatory response in the body and I believe as athletes we don't need any extra help in that department.

Prep Time: 10 minutes

Cook Time: 15 minutes

Servings: 6

Ingredients:

2 cups summer squash

2 cups zucchini

2 cups asparagus

1 12oz package of linguine (we like Bio-Nature for gluten-free)

Hemp Seed Pesto (recipe on page 87)

Preparation:

1. Preheat oven to 425 degrees.
2. Prepare hemp seed pesto.
3. Chop vegetables and roast on cookie sheet for 10 minutes, no oil necessary.
4. Cook pasta according to package directions.
5. Serve up with linguine as the base, top with roasted vegetables, pour pesto over top generously and get a spoon because you're gonna need it!

GOT THE MUNCHIES?

I'm very familiar with the munchies, and yes, for all the reasons you can imagine. It's just that now my munchie time comes as a result of pure, unadulterated movement of my body, a healthy metabolism and no longer a bong. I can hammer a bag of chips like nobody's business and there's been many a day that BJ and I exchange mind-blowing inspirations and stories while tortilla crumbs drop to the floor or final funnel "chipping" goes awry. It's truly a ridiculous situation for two people who are on a mission to create a better world. I mean are we really going to do that by mindlessly funneling dead food into our bodies? Instead, we remind ourselves that it is in fact about progress not perfection and that everything is a choice. We know very well that every time we choose one of these high vibe snacks over a milled corn triangle that the world will in fact be a better place.

CINNAMON YAM

Pierce the yam several times with a fork. Heat oven to 400 degrees and bake for 30-40 minutes, turn over about halfway through. Cooking time will depend on the size so stay close and check tenderness at the halfway point. This snack can be made the night before and reheated during your work day. Try it whole with a little coconut spread and cinnamon or mash it up and drizzle coconut milk over top.

Nutrition News: *Yams are high in vitamin A which is important to immune function while the cinnamon works with blood sugar regulation acting as the perfect complement to this sweet root vegetable.*

EDAMAME WITH ALMONDS

Cook shelled edamame according to the instructions on the bag, strain and pour into a bowl. Add chopped almonds, a drizzle of olive oil and salt to taste. Make up the entire bag and eat it over the course of a few days.

Nutrition News: *Edamame with almonds is high in protein, fiber, potassium, vitamin E and healthy fats. Best to buy organic edamame when possible, in the least look for a Non-GMO certified brand.*

AVOCADO QUINOA SMASH

Take 1/4 cup of your easy peasy, already chillin' in the fridge quinoa and add it to a bowl with 2 teaspoons of nutritional yeast. Cut a ripe avocado into small pieces and add to the quinoa then smash it all together. Add salt and pepper to taste. There's no shame in eating this straight out of the bowl. However, if you care to be more civilized serve on crackers or whole grain toast. Add spinach and tomato, make it a sandwich.

Nutrition News: Quinoa is a complete protein and it is a seed so if grains are not your favorite then quinoa will be. Avocados are a nutrient dense powerhouse; C, E, K, magnesium, potassium and omega-3 are all found in this vibrant green, single seeded berry.

PETRIFIED CARROTS

A snack named after our friend Petra who introduced us to this addicting crunch fest. Cut carrots into sticks, squeeze fresh lemon over top and a dash of salt. Toss together and snack away. This is a great salty, crunchy option for the chip lover.

Nutrition News: Carrots are loaded with beta-carotene and they increase saliva which releases digestive enzymes to make this crunchy friend not only delicious but easy on the belly.

FANCY PANTS SAUCES, DRESSINGS AND SPREADS

We're at a point in our plant-based adventure that a big ol' pile of plants is really all we need but that doesn't mean that we're going to deny that a nice dollop (or ten) of a totally banging sauce causes our buds to smile. How about that coconut banana bread in the dessert section of this book? Sure it's a life-changing bake but with its perfectly paired cacao hazelnut spread, it becomes a paradigm-shattering cake. These basic blends are multi-use for many meals and just good on their own. No preservatives and no added sugar, just straight up high vibe saucy love.

BALSAMIC CITRUS DRESSING

This dressing is super simple and the perfect combo of sweet and savory. A great complement to the Refreshingly Simple Spinach Salad in this book. Make this from scratch in minutes and you look like a hero!

Prep Time: 5 minutes

Cook Time: zero

Servings: 6

Ingredients:

¼ cup balsamic vinegar

¼ cup olive oil

⅛ cup juice from a ripe orange

¼ teaspoon orange zest

¼ teaspoon salt

¼ teaspoon black pepper

Preparation:

1. Combine in a small bowl and whisk together.

Chef Note: *If you don't have a microplane to zest the fruit then join the club because we don't either. I simply use the smallest option on my box grater or finely shaving the skin of the orange and dicing it up.*

LEMON THYME DRESSING

This is a solid all around dressing for salads, steamed veggies and a little extra taste for roasted potatoes, one of my favorite snacks. A good option for the spinach salad in this book if you're not digging the citrus of the recommended balsamic dressing.

Prep Time: 5 minutes

Cook Time: zero

Servings: 6

Ingredients:

½ cup fresh lemon juice (approximately one large lemon)

⅛ cup olive oil

1 teaspoon thyme dried or fresh thyme

¼ teaspoon lemon zest

½ teaspoon black pepper

¼ teaspoon salt

Preparation:

1. Combine in a small bowl and whisk together.

Chef Note: Don't sweat the zest if you don't have a microplane zest tool, life is so much easier when we just chill out so just dice up some delish lemon skin or use a traditional grater and call it a success.

SWEET CASHEW CREAM

Whipped cream lovers look no further because this is your new jam! A perfect topping to any dessert, bowl of fruit and especially our Cinnamon Breakfast Bake. Reference mindful eating section of this book to revisit chewing and presence, without this servings could easily be reduced to one.

Inactive Prep: 3 hours

Prep Time: 5 minutes

Cook Time: zero

Servings: 6-8

Ingredients:

1 cup of cashews, raw (soaked in water for at least 3 hours)

½ cup water

2 teaspoons vanilla extract

4 teaspoons maple syrup

Preparation:

1. Combine all ingredients in a high-powered blender. Blend low to high until silky smooth, approximately 1 minute.

AVOCADO TAHINI SAUCE

This multi-purpose sauce would make a great dressing for kale salad, topping for nachos or to up your burrito game. Whatever meal you serve it with keep it nearby for extra dollops.

Prep Time: 5 minutes

Cook Time: zero

Servings: 4-6

Ingredients:

1 ripe avocado, peeled and pitted

½ cup filtered water

¼ cup tahini

Zest and juice of 1 lemon

1 clove garlic

1 tablespoon apple cider vinegar

1 teaspoon cumin

⅛ teaspoon cayenne

Pinch of sea salt (optional)

Preparation:

1. Combine all ingredients in a high-powered blender or food processor until silky smooth. If you prefer a more liquid consistency slowly add more water, one tablespoon at a time.

ALMOND CHIPOTLE SAUCE

Two important things to heed with this super delish sauce: 1) it's not hummus, the base is almonds so similar to hummus it's high in protein, but not so similar, it's high in fat and 2) it packs fire so go easy on the chipotle peppers if heat is not your jam.

If you tend to be a feisty human already (take it from a recovering type A), then you may want to lower your external sources of fire all around. Otherwise, enjoy. This sauce is perfect for dressing up a simple black beans and brown rice night and of course, the perfect match to our jackfruit taco recipe. Also, a great dip for pita bread or tortilla chips. This recipe was inspired by Bitchin' Sauce, a local company that I was introduced to via our farmer's market.

Inactive Prep: 8-10 hours
Prep Time: 7 minutes
Cook Time: zero
Servings: 6-8

Ingredients:
1 cup raw almonds (soaked in water overnight, forgot that step? It's OK see tip below)
½ cup lemon juice (about 2 lemons)
¼ cup nutritional yeast
½ cup water
1 teaspoon sea or himalayan salt
2 tablespoons Bragg's Liquid Aminos (substitute with tamari or soy sauce)
3 plum tomatoes (chopped and seeded)
1 clove garlic
4-5 chipotle peppers (seeded, option to reduce amount-depending on your comfort level with heat)

Preparation:
1. Rinse and drain your almonds.
2. Combine all ingredients into a high-powered blender or food processor. Blend until smooth and creamy. Adjust seasonings to taste.

Chef Note: *Go easy on the peppers, add them one at a time and taste test to your preferred heat. Soaking Raw Almonds: If you didn't soak the night before, no worries. Soak in hot water for at least an hour, then drain.*

HEMP SEED PESTO

Back in my cheese-a-holic days one of my favorite sauces was pesto which is traditionally made with cheese, which is made from what Dr. Michael Klaper, from the documentary What the Health, describes as "baby calf growth fluid". Yup, that's gross and true. Alas, the curiosity of life that yoga has been known to cause got the best of my cheese addiction and within weeks I found myself dairy free, feeling better than ever before and on a quest to make a dairy free pesto. Voila!

Prep Time: 10 minutes
Cook Time: zero
Servings: 6

Ingredients:
4 cups basil leaves
¼ cup hemp seeds
¼ cup olive oil
⅛ cup lemon juice
½ teaspoon salt
1 clove garlic
1 tablespoon of crushed red pepper flakes

Preparation:
1. Remove basil from their stems and combine with the remaining ingredients in a high powered blender or food processor.

Chef Note: *If you want to stay low on the oil but need more moisture, slowly add filtered water by the tablespoon or more lemon juice.*

CACAO HAZELNUT SPREAD

This delish wonder spread confirms my proclivity for losing control. Chocolatey, nutty and creamy yet a little textured. This stuff is easy to put away with a spoon, standing in the kitchen, staring at the wall but my favorite way to enjoy it is spread generously on banana chips and no doubt as a frosting to our banana bread.

Prep Time: 15 minutes

Cook Time: 10 minutes

Servings: 12 ounces

Ingredients:

1 ½ cups hazelnuts (can't find hazelnuts or not in your budget? No sweat..any nut will do)

3 tablespoons cacao powder, unsweetened

¼ cup almond milk, unsweetened

¼ cup of maple syrup

1 tablespoon filtered water

1 teaspoon coconut oil, melted

1 teaspoon vanilla extract

pinch of sea salt

Preparation:

1. Heat oven to 350 degrees and toast hazelnuts for 8-10 minutes. Let them cool then peel the skins, they will come off easily, do it with love and intention.
2. Place nuts in a food processor or high-powered blender. Process until finely chopped.
3. Next add in your cacao powder and pulse to combine.
4. Add in your almond milk, maple syrup, water, coconut oil, vanilla and sea salt. Blend this to a thick buttery smooth consistency.
5. Spread onto cooled banana bread and top with coconut shreds or flakes. (optional)

SWEETS

COCONUT CHIA PUDDING

This is for the yogurt lovers. Breakfast, lunch, dinner or snack this coconut chia pudding never disappoints. Top with toasted coconut flakes, fresh berries or goji berries and cacao nibs for an extra punch of antioxidants and superfood flair. It's also good just by the spoonful for when you're on the run and need a few calories to get you there.

Inactive Prep: 1 hour

Prep Time: 5 minutes

Cook Time: zero

Servings: 4

Ingredients:

1 15-ounce can of coconut milk

3 teaspoons vanilla extract

3 tablespoons chia seeds

Preparation:

1. In a medium size mixing bowl, combine the coconut milk and vanilla. Depending on the brand of coconut milk there may be separation between solid and liquid, if this is the case then use a blender on low or use a hand mixer for 1-2 minutes.
2. Next add chia seeds to coconut milk vanilla mixture,stir to combine and cover tightly.
3. Store in fridge and allow to set at least 1 hour or up to overnight and enjoy.

Chef Note: *For a little more oomph add ½ of raw oats or cooked quinoa as the base when you serve it up.*

BANANA CACAO ICE CREAM

The options here are endless...lose the coconut, add frozen/fresh fruit into the blend, add vegan chocolate chips. Still concerned about where you're getting your protein? Skip the cacao and add a scoop of plant-based chocolate protein powder. Boom.

Inactive Prep Time: 2 hours

Prep Time: 5 minutes

Cook Time: zero

Servings: 1-2

Ingredients:

2 bananas, ripe and peeled then frozen for at least 2 hours

⅓ cup non-dairy milk, unsweetened

1 teaspoon vanilla extract

1 tablespoon cacao powder

1 tablespoon shredded coconut, unsweetened

Preparation:

1. Combine all ingredients in a high-powered blender, blend and enjoy!

ALMOND BUTTER DATES

My favorite before a long run and for testing my mindful eating abilities. I made these for our first plant-based workshop and they killed! Thinking, wishing I would have had more for leftovers, I went straight home to make my own stash that no one but me could eat. Thankfully BJ doesn't like these and I am grateful. Score one for marrying an opposite!

Prep Time: 10 minutes

Cook Time: zero

Servings: 10 stuffed dates

Ingredients:

10 medjool dates

½ cup almond butter

1 tablespoon cinnamon

¼ teaspoon sea salt

1 teaspoon chia seed

Preparation:

1. Combine almond butter with cinnamon and a pinch of sea salt.
2. Slice into the center of the date without cutting in half and remove the pit.
3. Spoon in almond butter mixture and top with a sprinkle of chia seeds.

Chef Note: *If you have extra almond butter, put it aside and use on toast with a drizzle of agave on top.*

COCONUT BANANA BREAD WITH HAZELNUT SPREAD

Let's go bananas for this anytime of day. You decide...breakfast, lunch, snack, training ride fuel or dessert. It's really your choice when to indulge in this dense loaf of love because frankly, it's good anytime! This homemade high vibe loaf was inspired by my mother in-law Teri and even though we've majorly tweaked the recipe, it still has all that great flavor and texture of the bread BJ grew up enjoying. Make and share this cruelty-free delight! You won't be disappointed.

Inactive Prep Time: 15 minutes
Prep Time: 30 minutes
Cook Time: 45-55 minutes
Servings: 1 loaf of bread

Ingredients:

1 tablespoon flaxseed, ground
3 tablespoons filtered water

Dry Ingredients:

2 ½ cups of old fashioned oats OR 2 cups of oat flour
½ teaspoon baking soda
1 ½ teaspoon baking powder
1 teaspoon salt
½ teaspoon cinnamon
½ teaspoon nutmeg
¼ cup walnuts, chopped

Wet Ingredients:

5 bananas, very ripe and mashed
3 tablespoons applesauce, unsweetened
6 Medjool dates soaked in filtered water for 10-15 minutes or 2 tablespoons of date paste
¼ cup coconut oil, melted

Continued on next page

COCONUT BANANA BREAD WITH HAZELNUT SPREAD

Toppings:

Cacao Hazelnut Spread (recipe on page 89)

2 tablespoons shredded coconut, unsweetened

Preparation:

1. Preheat oven to 350 degrees and lightly grease a loaf size pan with coconut oil.

2. In a small bowl combine ground flaxseeds and water, stir and set in refrigerator for 15 minutes.* In another bowl begin to soak your dates

3. Next prepare your oatmeal. If using old fashioned rolled oats, blend in food processor or high powered blender until you reach a flour-like consistency. (We tend to keep ours a little rough for extra texture) The 2 ½ cups of oats should yield 2 cups of flour. If using packaged oat flour, just measure and add to mixing bowl.

4. Place oat flour into a large mixing bowl and add baking powder, baking soda and spices. Stir to combine and set aside.

5. In another medium-size mixing bowl combine mashed bananas, flaxseed-water mixture, melted coconut oil, applesauce.

6. Rough chop the dates, too about the size of raisins then add to wet ingredients.**

7. Add wet ingredients to dry and stir to combine. Fold in chopped walnuts and pour batter into prepared loaf pan. Cook for 55-60 minutes, depending on your oven. Keep your eye on it and check after 40-45 minutes. Bread should smell amazing, be firm to touch and a toothpick should come out clean from the middle of the loaf. Don't have toothpicks? No worries, I've been using very small sticks I find in the bushes, just wipe them clean and they work like a charm.

8. Allow bread to cool in loaf pan for 10 minutes, then remove from pan and leave to cool completely on a wire rack.

9. Once cooled, frost with Cacao Hazelnut Spread and top with shredded coconut. Or horizontally cut the loaf in half and layer the spread and coconut shreds in between the upper and lower halves for the best banana bread sandwich of your life! Grab a big mug of tea or coffee and prepare to eat mindfully because this plant-based paradise has been known to get the best of the most mindful high-viber.

Continued on next page

COCONUT BANANA BREAD WITH HAZELNUT SPREAD

Chef Note:

Flaxseed mixture acts as a binder or 'egg' in your banana bread.

**If you are the adventurous type, you can make date paste by following the instructions below. This particular recipe would call for 2 tablespoons of date paste mixed in with wet ingredients.

Making your own Date Paste!
If you're channeling your inner Julia Child and want to make your own sweet date paste from whole foods...we totally understand and respect that. Here's how we make ours.

Begin by pitting and soaking 6 large Medjool dates in a bowl of filtered water. Let them soak for minutes until soft. Once soaked blend them with ¼ cup of water in a high-powered blender or food processor until smooth paste is formed. You might need to stop a few times to scrape down the sides. And if the mixture is too thick, just add more water-one tablespoon at a time. And voilà....homemade date paste is born!

You'll definitely have extra date paste so continue to use it as a sugar substitute or make "caramel" apples by rolling the apples in the date paste then in shredded coconut. Boom!

PLANT-BASED POOCHES

There are many dogs who thrive on a vegan diet and Clark is one of those lucky pups. However, it's important to note that Clark was not always thriving on a vegan diet. We had him on a dry vegan kibble for almost a year when it became clear that he was not as vibrant as he should have been at two years old. He was 10 pounds overweight and lethargic. It didn't matter that I increased his exercise and decreased his food intake, he was not losing weight or feeling spry.

Dry kibble is convenient but not ideal for high level health. Plain and simple, it's a processed food. Imagine how would you feel if you ate a bowl of cereal for breakfast and dinner everyday, for the rest of your life.

I knew in my heart it was the food and there was no doubt in my mind, I had to step up my game for Clark. It was super important to exhaust the plant-based options before moving towards an animal based diet for him. Despite our vet threatening not to care for Clark anymore if he remained vegan, I set off on a quest to educate myself on his behalf. His health is the #1 concern and I was not putting hard lmiits on his future, I just felt compelled to act in alignment with my values as the first step. Lucky for Clark and the animals that become dog food, we have found another way.

Enter Michelle, a woman I'm so grateful to call a friend. She showed up in my life at the exact right time. She had just completed the formulation of Benji's Canine Cuisine, a human grade, vegan dog food in honor of her lost four-legged soul mate, Benji. We met for coffee and she had all the answers to my questions. I left with knowledge and a plan to assist Clark in living to his potential. Game on!

This is the basic recipe that Michelle helped me compile based on Clark's goal weight and activity level. Clark loved it from first bite and it was just what I needed to have the confidence to create his food in my kitchen, under my control and from my heart. I'm happy to say Clark is at his goal weight and we're continuing to find our plant-prep groove.

The following recipe comes in just under 1,000 calories. Our Clark weighs 66 pounds. We figured out that he requires around 1,700-2,000 calories a day to maintain his healthy weight. There are several resources online to help calculate this for your own plant pooch. I found however, that the calculations differ greatly depending on the source so just like with my own body, I monitor him closely for feedback.

Here's our Clark approved Pooch Pooridge....made with extra love.

POOCH POORIDGE

Ingredients:

1 cup cooked millet

2 cups of filtered water

1 cup mashed sweet potatoes

¼ cup fortified non-dairy milk

1 cup pureed broccoli

1 cup pureed peas

1 tablespoon nutritional yeast

1 tablespoon turmeric

Black pepper

Preparation:

1. Preheat oven to 400 degrees
2. Bring 2 cups of filtered water to a boil and add 1 cup of dry millet. Cover and simmer for 15 minutes.
3. Wash and poke sweet potatoes several times with a fork (this will help them cook faster) OR cut sweet potatoes into small cubes and bake on a small cookie sheet. Bake potatoes for 50-60 minutes depending on their size. Make sure they are very soft, combine with non-dairy milk and mash them with a fork or potato masher.**
4. Rough chop a crown of broccoli and steam with the peas for 7 minutes.***
5. Combine vegetables in a blender of food processor with a bit of the water they were steamed with and puree.
6. Combine designated measurements above if he/she is Clark's size or adjust to your fur baby's caloric needs. Mix everything together with the spices in your pup's bowl and serve up.

Chef's Note:

Make a big quantity of millet and store in tupperware or freeze for another day. This is people food too and very healthy so ask your pup if it's ok that you share in the goodness too.

Microwaves are a timesaver for cooking the veggies and potatoes. Don't kill yourself trying to do it all, enjoy the shortcuts of our modern world and use the extra time to chew your food.

If you are using fresh broccoli use the stems and all. A good shortcut is buying frozen vegetables, nutrition is high and the convenience level is even higher.

Nutrition News: *The fortified non-dairy milk is for extra nutrients, nutritional yeast is for B-12, ground flax meal for the omegas, turmeric is a potent anti-inflammatory and the black pepper helps to activate the healing properties of the turmeric.*

Made in the USA
Lexington, KY
02 March 2018